Date: 6/13/13

BR ANDREWS
Andrews, Alexa.
At the beach /

Dear Parents and Educators,

Welcome to Penguin Young Readers! As parents and educators, you know that each child develops at his or her own pace—in terms of speech, critical thinking, and, of course, reading. Penguin Young Readers recognizes this fact. As a result, each Penguin Young Readers book is assigned a traditional easy-to-read level (1–4) as well as a Guided Reading Level (A–P). Both of these systems will help you choose the right book for your child. Please refer to the back of each book for specific leveling information. Penguin Young Readers features esteemed authors and illustrators, stories about favorite characters, fascinating nonfiction, and more!

At the Beach

LEVEL **1**

GUIDED
READING
LEVEL **A**

This book is perfect for an **Emergent Reader** who:
• can read in a left-to-right and top-to-bottom progression;
• can recognize some beginning and ending letter sounds;
• can use picture clues to help tell the story; and
• can understand the basic plot and sequence of simple stories.

Here are some **activities** you can do during and after reading this book:
• Phrase Repetition: Reread the story and count how many times you read the following phrases: *in the water, on the sand*, and *at the beach.* How many objects do you find in each place? How many animals? Have you seen all the objects and animals named?
• Make Connections: Each of the three sections in this book name different objects and animals one would likely find in the water, on the sand, and at the beach. Take a look at each section again and brainstorm other things one might see. For fun, have the child draw a picture of the object or animal, while the parent/caregiver writes down the word.

Remember, sharing the love of reading with a child is the best gift you can give!

—Bonnie Bader, EdM
Penguin Young Readers program

*Penguin Young Readers are leveled by independent reviewers applying the standards developed by Irene Fountas and Gay Su Pinnell in *Matching Books to Readers: Using Leveled Books in Guided Reading*, Heinemann, 1999.

To my amazing mom, who always had time to take us to the beach, even if it happened to be a cold, seaweed-filled Minnesota lake—CK

Penguin Young Readers
Published by the Penguin Group
Penguin Group (USA) Inc., 375 Hudson Street, New York, New York 10014, USA
Penguin Group (Canada), 90 Eglinton Avenue East, Suite 700, Toronto, Ontario M4P 2Y3, Canada
(a division of Pearson Penguin Canada Inc.)
Penguin Books Ltd, 80 Strand, London WC2R 0RL, England
Penguin Ireland, 25 St Stephen's Green, Dublin 2, Ireland (a division of Penguin Books Ltd)
Penguin Group (Australia), 707 Collins Street, Melbourne, Victoria 3008, Australia
(a division of Pearson Australia Group Pty Ltd)
Penguin Books India Pvt Ltd, 11 Community Centre, Panchsheel Park, New Delhi—110 017, India
Penguin Group (NZ), 67 Apollo Drive, Rosedale, Auckland 0632, New Zealand
(a division of Pearson New Zealand Ltd)
Penguin Books (South Africa), Rosebank Office Park, 181 Jan Smuts Avenue,
Parktown North 2193, South Africa
Penguin China, B7 Jiaming Center, 27 East Third Ring Road North,
Chaoyang District, Beijing 100020, China

Penguin Books Ltd, Registered Offices: 80 Strand, London WC2R 0RL, England

Photo credits: cover: (crab) © Hemera/Thinkstock, (birds, beach ball) © iStockphoto/Thinkstock, (sand castles) © Photodisc/Thinkstock, ; cover, page 3: (bucket, shovel) © iStockphoto/Thinkstock; page 6–13,16–23, 26–32: (sun) © Comstock/Thinkstock, page 5: © iStockphoto/Thinkstock; page 6: © iStockphoto/Thinkstock; page 7: © iStockphoto/Thinkstock; page 8: © iStockphoto/Thinkstock; page 9: © iStockphoto/Thinkstock; page 10: © iStockphoto/Thinkstock; page 11: © iStockphoto/Thinkstock; page 12: © Zoonar/Thinkstock; page 13: © iStockphoto/Thinkstock; page 15: © Hemera/Thinkstock; page 16: (top shell) © Hemera/Thinkstock, (rest of shells) © iStockphoto/Thinkstock; page 17: (top beach ball) © Stockbyte/Thinkstock, (rest of beach balls) © iStockphoto/Thinkstock; page 18: © Hemera/Thinkstock; page 19: © PhotoObjects.net/Thinkstock; page 20: (green, red, blue towels) © iStockphoto/Thinkstock, (orange towel) © Goodshoot/Thinkstock; page 21: © iStockphoto/Thinkstock; page 22: © iStockphoto/Thinkstock; page 23: (top surfboard) © Comstock/Thinkstock, (rest of surfboards) © Hemera/Thinkstock; page 25: © Zoonar/Thinkstock; page 26: © Photodisc/Thinkstock; page 27: (flying birds and middle bird on sand) © iStockphoto/Thinkstock, (top and bottom bird on sand) © Hemera/Thinkstock; page 28: (top sand castle) © Photodisc/Thinkstock, (bottom sand castle) © iStockphoto/Thinkstock; page 29: © iStockphoto/Thinkstock; page 30: © iStockphoto/Thinkstock; page 31: © iStockphoto/Thinkstock; page 32.

Library of Congress Cataloging-in-Publication Data is available.

ISBN 978-0-448-46471-8 (pbk)
ISBN 978-0-448-46570-8 (hc)

10 9 8 7 6 5 4 3 2 1
10 9 8 7 6 5 4 3 2 1

At the Beach

by Alexa Andrews
illustrated by Candice Keimig
and with photographs

Penguin Young Readers
An Imprint of Penguin Group (USA) Inc.

In the Water

Fish live in the water.

Dolphins live in the water.

Sharks live in the water.

Whales live in the water.

Turtles live in the water.

Jellyfish live in the water.

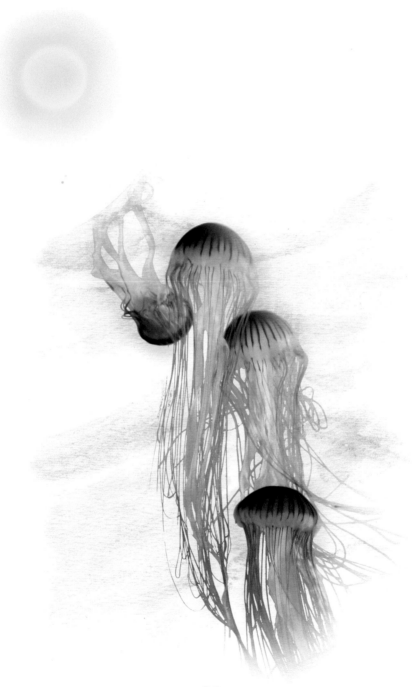

Starfish live in the water.

Clams live in the water.

On the Sand

Shells are on the sand.

Beach balls are on the sand.

Crabs are on the sand.

Buckets are on the sand.

Towels are on the sand.

Sunglasses are on the sand.

Beach chairs are on the sand.

Surfboards are on the sand.

At the Beach

Umbrellas are at the beach.

Birds are at the beach.

Sand castles are at the beach.

Trees are at the beach.

Kites are at the beach.

Bags are at the beach.

The sun is at the beach.